Alabama
The Heart of Dixie

Marcia Amidon Lusted

PowerKiDS press™

New York

Published in 2010 by The Rosen Publishing Group, Inc.
29 East 21st Street, New York, NY 10010

First Edition

Editor: Nicole Pristash
Book Layout: Julio Gil
Book Design: Greg Tucker
Photo Researcher: Jessica Gerweck

Photo Credits: Cover © Fred Hirschmann/Science Faction/Corbis; p. 5 © www.iStockphoto.com/Perry Watson; p. 7 © Tom Till/age fotostock; p. 7 (inset) Archive Photos/Getty Images; p. 9 William Lovelace/ Express/Getty Images; pp. 11, 15 © Jeff Greenberg/age fotostock; pp. 13, 22 (bird) © Wayne Lynch/ age fotostock; pp. 17, 22 (tree, bear, flag, flower) Shutterstock.com; p. 19 Christian Petersen/Getty Images; p. 22 (Helen Keller) New York Times Co./Getty Images; p. 22 (Rosa Parks) William Philpott/ Getty Images; p. 22 (Terrell Owens) Lisa Blumenfeld/Getty Images.

Library of Congress Cataloging-in-Publication Data

Lusted, Marcia Amidon.
  Alabama : the Heart of Dixie / Marcia Amidon Lusted. — 1st ed.
     p. cm. — (Our amazing states)
  Includes index.
  ISBN 978-1-4358-9349-8 (library binding) — ISBN 978-1-4358-9792-2 (pbk.) — ISBN 978-1-4358-9793-9 (6-pack)
  1. Alabama—Juvenile literature. I. Title.
  F326.3.L87 2010
  976.1—dc22
                                           2009028720

Manufactured in the United States of America

CPSIA Compliance Information: Batch #WW10PK: For Further Information contact Rosen Publishing, New York, New York at 1-800-237-9932

Contents

Heart of Dixie

There is a state that has seen American history unfold during the **civil rights movement**. It is a state where magnolia trees grow and jazz music can be heard. Where are we? We are in Alabama! Alabama is one of America's southern states. It is located between Georgia and Mississippi, and Florida is south of the state. A small part of Alabama touches the Gulf of Mexico, where the Mobile River **drains** into Mobile Bay.

One of Alabama's nicknames is the Heart of Dixie. Dixieland is a nickname for the southern part of the United States. Because Montgomery, Alabama, was the first capital of the **Confederacy**, Alabama became known as the Heart of Dixie.

Oak trees, tall fountains, and colorful flowers are common sights in the South. Here they are seen in Bienville Square, a park in downtown Mobile, Alabama.

From Mounds to Statehood

People lived in what is now Alabama as far back as 12,000 years ago. Early groups made shelters out of rock found in the area. Years later, Native Americans known as the Woodland people built large dirt mounds there that served as temples or burial places.

In 1519, the Spanish became the first Europeans to explore Alabama. In 1702, the French came and built Fort Louis de La Louisiane, on the Mobile River. Settlers from France cleared the land for farms and began using African slaves for labor. France, Great Britain, and Spain each had control over parts of the area at one point until the late 1700s, when the United States gained it all. Alabama became the twenty-second state in 1819.

The mounds shown here were built between 1000 and 1450. *Inset:* Hernando de Soto was one of the first Spanish explorers to visit Alabama.

Taking a Stand

The civil rights movement of the 1950s and 1960s is an important part of U.S. history, and Alabama played a big part in it. In 1955, an African-American woman named Rosa Parks was arrested in Montgomery because she would not give up her seat on a bus to a white man. By law, blacks had to give their seats to white passengers on crowded buses. Many people felt that this was unfair. Parks's arrest sparked a **boycott** of the city's buses. This increased awareness of the civil rights movement.

During the movement, people **demonstrated** against **segregation** in Birmingham. In 1965, hundreds of people marched from Selma to Montgomery to **protest** the treatment of blacks. Alabama is rich with history from this important time.

On March 25, 1965, the Selma to Montgomery march ended at the Alabama State Capitol Building, shown here. Around 25,000 people gathered there to protest.

Rivers and Hurricanes

Alabama is shaped a little like a rectangle. From the northeastern part of the state, where the Appalachian Mountains begin, Alabama's land slopes down toward the western and southern parts of the state. The south-central area of Alabama, called the Black Belt, has rich soil. Farmers once built large cotton **plantations** there. The southern part of the state is flat.

Alabama has many rivers. The Alabama River and the Tombigbee River are two of its major rivers.

Alabama has hot, humid summers and warm winters. **Hurricanes** with high winds and rain often occur there, and once in a while it may snow in the northern part of the state.

This is the Holt Lock and Dam on the Black Warrior River. This dam has a hydroelectric plant, or a place that uses water to create power for surrounding cities.

Alabama Wildlife

One of Alabama's other nicknames is the Yellowhammer State. The yellowhammer is Alabama's state bird. During the **Civil War**, soldiers from Alabama were often called yellowhammers. Soon, this nickname was used for the whole state. Alabama is also home to alligators, opossums, minks, and otters. Catfish and flounder swim through its waters, and fishermen catch shrimp and oysters in them. They have to watch out for poisonous coral snakes and water moccasins, though!

Red cedar, black walnut, southern pine, and sweet gum trees are a few of the trees that grow in Alabama's forests. Asters, black-eyed Susans, and wild blue indigo wildflowers grow there, too. Alabama's state flower is the camellia.

The yellowhammer, shown here, is also known as the yellow-shafted flicker.

Made in Alabama

Many of the things that you use every day may have been made in Alabama. From clothing to paper, many different types of companies have factories in the state. Cars and **electronics** are made there, too. Alabama farmers grow pecans, sweet potatoes, and tomatoes. Half the peanuts in the United States are grown in Alabama! Other farmers in the state raise chickens and beef cattle. Fishermen catch crabs, oysters, and mussels.

Many **tourists** come to Alabama, especially along the Gulf Coast, so a lot of people have jobs working in restaurants and hotels there. Many people work for the government at Marshall Space Flight Center, in Huntsville, and the Maxwell-Gunter Air Force Base, in Montgomery.

This farmer is checking her crop at a cotton farm in Gaylesville, Alabama. In 2007, there were 382,586 acres (154,827 ha) of cotton farms in the state.

Alabama's Capital

Alabama's capital city is Montgomery. It is located near the center of the state. More than 200,000 people live there.

If you are looking for something interesting to do in Montgomery, you can visit the MOOseum, where you can learn more about the beef cattle business in Alabama. There is a **planetarium** and a zoo in the city, too. If you enjoy the outdoors, you can take a boat ride on the Alabama River, see the Montgomery Biscuits play a baseball game, or hear a concert at the Riverwalk **Amphitheater**. Visitors to Montgomery can also learn more about the civil rights movement at the Rosa Parks Museum and Library and the Civil Rights Memorial Center.

The Alabama State Capitol Building was built in 1851. The land on which the building sits is known as Goat Hill because goat pastures once covered the area.

The Fast Track

One of the most famous racetracks in America started off as a field next to a few empty airplane runways. Today, the Talladega Superspeedway, in eastern Alabama, is one of the biggest and best racetracks in the world. It covers almost 5 square miles (13 sq km)! The track itself is almost 3 miles (5 km) long, and 143,000 people can watch races from the stands.

Many NASCAR races are held at Talladega every year. The track holds the record for the fastest 500-mile (805 km) stock-car race ever. In 1997, the winning car reached 188 miles per hour (303 km/h)! There are also driving schools at Talladega, where people can learn what it is like to drive a race car.

This picture shows the 2009 Aaron's 499 NASCAR race at Talladega Superspeedway. Driver Brad Keselowski won this race.

Come to Alabama!

There are many reasons why Alabama is an amazing state. One reason is Little River Canyon National Preserve, near Fort Payne, where visitors can go camping and bird-watch. While they are there, they can also see some of the South's most beautiful waterfalls, such as the 45-foot-(14 m) high Little River Falls. Visitor can also go to the U.S. Space and Rocket Center, in Huntsville, where they can see rocket parts being built or attend a space camp. There is even a full-size space shuttle on display there!

Alabama has many interesting places to visit. It is also a nice place to live, whether you like cities or quiet places, the mountains or the ocean. Come to Alabama!

Glossary

amphitheater (AMP-fuh-thee-eh-ter) A large, open-air building with rows of seats in a high circle around an arena.

boycott (BOY-kot) A refusal to deal with a person or a business.

civil rights movement (SIH-vul RYTS MOOV-mint) People and groups working together to win freedom and equality for all.

Civil War (SIH-vul WOR) The war fought between the Northern and the Southern states of America from 1861 to 1865.

Confederacy (kun-FEH-duh-reh-see) The 11 Southern states that announced that they were separating themselves from the United States in 1860 and 1861.

demonstrated (DEH-mun-strayt-ed) Spoke up in public for a cause.

drains (DRAYNZ) Moves by natural paths.

electronics (ih-lek-TRAH-niks) Objects that are powered by electricity.

hurricanes (HUR-ih-kaynz) Storms with strong winds and heavy rain.

planetarium (pla-nih-TER-ee-um) A theater with a domed screen on top used for looking at pictures of the night sky.

plantations (plan-TAY-shunz) Very large farms where crops are grown.

protest (pruh-TEST) To act in disagreement.

segregation (seh-grih-GAY-shun) The act of keeping people of one race, sex, or social class away from others.

tourists (TUR-ists) People visiting a place where they do not live.

Alabama State Symbols

State Tree
Southern Longleaf Pine

State Animal
Black Bear

State Flag

State Bird
Yellowhammer

State Flower
Camellia

State Seal

Famous People from Alabama

Helen Keller
(1880–1968)
Born in Tuscumbia, AL
Author/Educator

Rosa Parks
(1913–2005)
Born in Tuskegee, AL
Civil Rights Leader

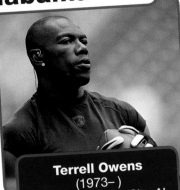
Terrell Owens
(1973–)
Born in Alexander City, AL
Football Player

22

Alabama State Map

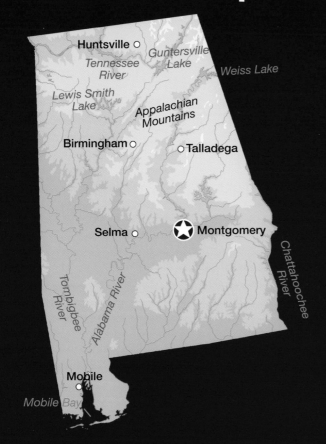

Legend

○ Major City

✪ Capital

∿ *River*

Alabama State Facts

Population: About 4,447,355

Area: 51,705 square miles (133,915 sq km)

Motto: "Audemus jura nostra defendere" ("We dare defend our rights")

Song: "Alabama," words by Julia S. Tutwiler and music by
Edna Gockel Gussen

Index

Web Sites

Due to the changing nature of Internet links, PowerKids Press has developed an online list of Web sites related to the subject of this book. This site is updated regularly. Please use this link to access the list:
www.powerkidslinks.com/amst/al/